Trains

By Hal Rogers

The Child's World®, Inc.

Published by The Child's World®, Inc.
PO Box 326
Chanhassen, MN 55317-0326
800-599-READ
www.childsworld.com

Design and Production:
The Creative Spark, San Juan Capistrano, CA

Photos: © 2000 David M. Budd Photography

Library of Congress Cataloging-in-Publication Data

Rogers, Hal.
   Trains / by Hal Rogers.
      p. cm.
   ISBN 1-56766-965-4
   1. Railroads—Juvenile literature. [1. Railroads—Trains.] I. Title.
 TF148 .R65 2001
 385—dc21
                                              00-011374

Contents

On the Job

On the job, trains carry people and **freight** from place to place. Trains have **locomotives** that pull cars behind them.

Trains have metal wheels that roll

along metal railroad tracks.

Sometimes trains travel through
tunnels. A tunnel is a long hole dug
through a hill or mountain.

This freight train carries coal. Other trains carry big things, such as cars and trucks. Trains even carry mail from city to city.

People travel on **passenger** trains. Each
car has a door where the people may
board. Passengers must have tickets to
ride the train. The **conductor** collects
their tickets.

Another worker takes care of the passengers' suitcases. He puts the suitcases in the **baggage car.**

Passenger cars have many seats. On long trips, people eat their meals on the train. They can visit a special dining car to order food.

The conductor helps connect two train cars. Train cars are connected with **couplers.** These strong hooks hold the cars together, no matter how fast the train goes.

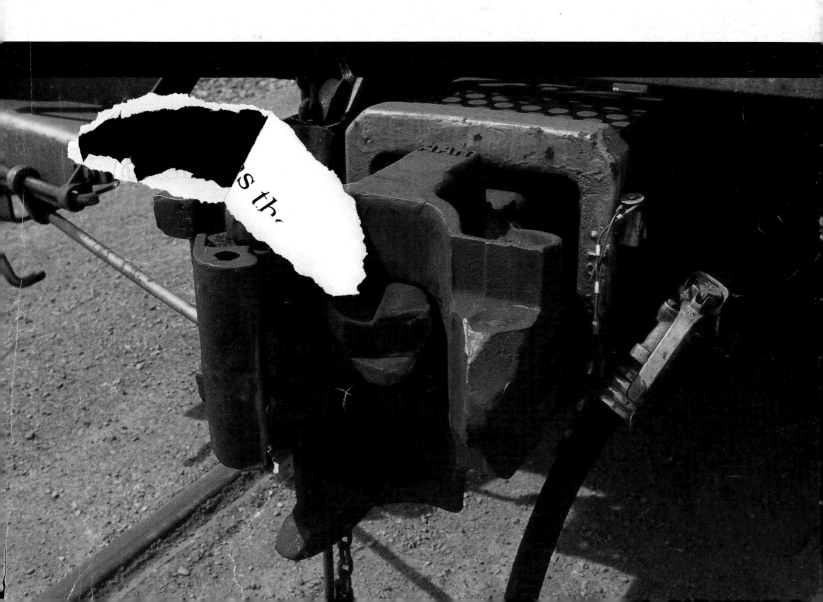

Trains once had a **caboose.** It was the small car at the end of a train. Today few trains have a caboose.

The last car on a train has a flashing red light. It helps people see the train.

Climb Aboard!

Would you like to see where the driver sits?

The driver of a train is called an **engineer.**

The engineer sits in the **cab.** The cab is inside

the locomotive. There are many **controls** in

the cab. The engineer has a special telephone.

It is called a **radio.** The engineer uses the

radio to talk to other workers.

Up Close

The inside

1. The radio

2. The controls

3. The engineer's seat

The outside

Glossary

baggage car (BAG-edj KAR)
A baggage car is a special car on a train where suitcases and other large items are stored.

board (BORD)
When people board a train, they get on it. Passenger cars have doors where people may board.

cab (KAB)
A cab is where a train's engineer sits. The cab has many controls and a seat for the engineer.

caboose (kuh-BOOS)
A caboose is a small car at the end of a train. Train workers once rode in cabooses.

conductor (kun-DUK-tur)
A conductor is a worker in charge of a train. The conductor helps connect train cars and takes passengers' tickets.

controls (kun-TROLZ)
Controls are buttons, switches, and other tools that make a machine work. The engineer uses controls to run the train.

couplers (CUP-lerz)
Couplers are giant hooks used to connect train cars. The conductor connects the couplers.

engineer (en-jih-NEER)
An engineer is a person who drives a train. The engineer sits in the cab.

freight (FRAYT)
Freight is something that a train carries. A freight train can carry coal, mail, or other things.

locomotives (loh-koh-MOH-tivz)
Locomotives are giant engines that move trains. Locomotives pull or push other railroad cars along the tracks.

passenger (PASS-en-jer)
A passenger is a traveler in a vehicle such as a bus, car, train, or airplane. Many people ride on passenger trains.

radio (RAY-dee-oh)
A radio lets people talk back and forth without wires. The engineer uses a radio to talk to workers in another car or at the station.